PUT TIME
—— *on* ——
YOUR SIDE

Jack Sutherland

PUT TIME

on

YOUR SIDE

How to Achieve Financial
Independence in Retirement

Jack Sutherland

PUT TIME ON YOUR SIDE
HOW TO ACHIEVE FINANCIAL INDEPENDENCE
IN RETIREMENT

iUniverse books may be ordered through booksellers or by contacting:

iUniverse
1663 Liberty Drive
Bloomington, IN 47403
www.iuniverse.com
1-800-Authors (1-800-288-4677)

ISBN: 978-1-4917-9783-9 (sc)
ISBN: 978-1-4917-9789-1 (e)

Library of Congress Control Number: 2016908920

Print information available on the last page.

iUniverse rev. date: 08/11/2016

DEDICATED TO

COLINE, JENNIFER, SARA AND MARK

Contents

Introduction

Survey after survey indicates how financially ill prepared most Americans are for retirement. This casual approach to the last twenty, thirty, or forty years of life manifests itself in the majority of working adults being clueless about how to finance retirement after the end of their careers. It also includes lack of a written plan, inadequate saving, and no idea how much money it will take to live the lives they want in retirement.

This is a scenario I want you to avoid. You can be retirement-planning literate with the help of this book about money and the steps leading to your financial independence in retirement. *Put Time on Your Side* is one person's story, but it contains the elements of every adult's quest to provide a financially secure retirement. Let's start with a brief history of money.

Money has been the source of conflict within families and among friends for centuries. The history of money reflects both joy and discontent. Money has played an important role in people's lives since very early civilization. Metal coins were used in Lydia (now western Turkey) around 600 BC. Paper currency appeared in China as early as AD 960. For the past three thousand years, some form of money has been the accepted method of payment for goods and services. Before money, a barter system existed using commodities and animals as the primary value units. Since 1862, paper currency has been in circulation in the United States.

Money has been both timely and timeless, and it continues to be a significant preoccupation for many people. Too many people know so little about saving and investing that they are not able to provide for their financial security in retirement. Separate yourself from this group. You can avoid this retirement conundrum by following the simple strategies outlined in this book and getting started when you put time on your side.

For me, the very thought of running out of money in retirement or being dependent on others to care for and support me in my later years has been a strong motivation for me to build a retirement strategy. I have accomplished this in real time. This book is about a practical and proven approach to building financial independence in retirement.

It has been said that success is getting what you want and happiness is wanting what you get. I can honestly say I am happy with the success I have experienced with my investment and retirement planning. Could I have done better? Sure, but life happens, and before you know it, the paychecks stop and you are retired, living on the dividends and interest from your investments. I only hope you will feel the same sense of satisfaction and achievement about your journey toward retirement. After all, that is the whole point of this book.

I have organized this book around sixteen chapters that cover the topics I believe are most relevant in planning for and achieving financial independence. I have also included thirty-eight specific strategies to turn these topics into a realistic plan of action. These topics and strategies are derived from lessons I have learned during a lifetime of financial experience. I intend for this information to help you prepare for a secure retirement. This book will be of little help if you are already living in retirement. This is not an exhaustive research study on preparing for retirement. This book should be used as a guide to explore various strategies that ultimately can contribute to a successful retirement plan.

Qualifications of the Author

Advanced degrees in business; a long, successful career; and the discipline to follow my personal financial plan combine to qualify me to write on this topic. My educational background includes a BS in finance and banking and an MBA in finance, supplemented with a career spanning more than forty years in commercial banking and twenty-five years as a community bank president and the development of my personal retirement plan. I have owned my own business, and I am the managing partner in a privately owned financial-services business. These qualifications provide me with a unique perspective for helping you achieve financial independence in retirement.

Chapter 1

Early Childhood Reflections

Achieving financial independence in retirement has been my goal for as long as I can remember. My parents did it. My grandparents did it. Why not me? Does it require luck, inheritance, fate, hard work, or some combination of all four to arrive at retirement with adequate funding? I don't think we should live in a world of either-or choices. For me, a combination of planning, hard work, and investing formed the foundation of my retirement planning. These were my observations in trying to understand why some people make and save more money than others.

I grew up in Lamar, Missouri, as the youngest in a middle-class family of five. I had some type of part-time job from the age of eight. I was expected to earn my spending money and save for future goals like buying a bike or a baseball glove, going to college, and making future investments. My parents were savers, not investors. The difference will become clear later.

From a long list of early jobs—including sweeping the stairs for a local law firm, having a paper route for the *Daily Democrat*, mowing lawns and shoveling coal for Mrs. Spencer in the winter, driving a truck and delivering fresh milk to families from a local dairy, and working summers on my grandparents' farm—I found that making money was hard work. I knew that hard work alone would only get me so far, so I devised a plan that over time would combine my willingness to work with a commitment to financial discipline focused on achieving financial independence.

Strategy #1: Setting Goals

If you do not know where you want to go, how do you get there? Goal setting has always been an important part of how I address future-planning challenges. Some have said I have a quick 1-2-3 answer for just about anything. Without goals, I think people go through life just reacting to whatever happens to them and around them. I describe a lack of goal setting as just responding to the next phone call, e-mail, or text message.

Most successful people I know have been planners and goal setters. Success is a choice. Decide what your goals are, make conscious decisions to move you along the path toward achieving them, and make every day count.

Ready, fire, aim? This is how some people approach planning. They make many impulse decisions that satisfy their wants but leave their basic need for retirement planning and execution still wanting. Good planning can help you avoid some impulse purchases—if you only take time to think about it. Get serious about planning because it is a serious subject that will affect your future. You cannot win a race if there is no finish line. Your plan can chart your personal course of action.

To set a financial goal, start with the desired end result, and then break that number down into smaller amounts for annual and monthly contributions. For example, if you want to save $100,000 in a cash reserve account by age sixty-five and your current age is thirty, then you have thirty-five years to achieve your desired results. Dividing $100,000 by thirty-five gives you an amount needed to save annually of $2,860. Divide this by twelve, and you have a monthly amount to save of $240. The monthly amount sounds more achievable. These numbers are without the benefit of earning interest.

Strategy #2: Save something from every paycheck.

During eighth grade, I became interested in business, and this led me to explore banking. Bankers in my small town were respected for their community involvement, leadership positions in the city, involvement in company board of director activities, and their apparent overall understanding of financial matters. These traits translated into helping people meet their business and personal financial goals.

My grandfather had been instrumental in the founding of a bank in Lamar, Missouri. He personally helped the Lamar bank survive the Depression. He was not a banker; he was a farmer who had come to the United States from Switzerland at the age of fourteen with his parents and started farming in Barton County, Missouri. He was my hero for all he accomplished with his hard work and dedication to his family. His was a frugal lifestyle. His family of seven was self-sufficient with gardens, orchards, livestock, chickens, and crops raised on the farm using their own labor. He believed strongly in hard work and saving. Out of every dollar earned, he always saved something. This was the savings philosophy he passed along to me. It is what made him a successful farmer and businessman and earned him the respect of others within the community. I have tried to follow this philosophy throughout my life, and I hope I have passed it along to my children. My grandfather passed away when I was in the sixth grade, and it was one of the saddest days of my life.

Strategy #3: Endorse the concept of saving.

What is the difference between saving and investing? They are intertwined; it is impossible to invest if you have not saved. Savings should be a risk-free activity. Putting aside money in money market accounts, bank certificates of deposit, or other insured, protected accounts is a form of savings. These are funds you cannot afford to lose or have decline in value. Rainy day funds (funds saved for emergencies or hard times) are best maintained in these types of accounts. Because these accounts have little risk, their yield is very low. Remember—risk and reward are related: the higher the risk, the higher the potential reward or yield should be.

My parents saved by using risk-free products like FDIC-insured bank deposit accounts. They provided for their financial independence by avoiding risk. They both lived through the Depression of the 1930s and had no tolerance for taking risks with their hard-earned money. I admired their financial discipline and success.

Strategy #4: Investing adds risk, but potential returns can be improved.

Investing, by its very nature, involves risk. Investments offer the opportunity to grow your savings at a faster rate than bank deposit accounts. Balancing risk with the expected return is always the first step to investing.

Types of Investment Products

Equities: This includes common stock and mutual fund shares. The shares represent ownership units in a mutual fund, and common stock represents ownership in an individual company.

Fixed Income: This includes bonds, mortgages, and other investments with a fixed interest rate.

Mutual Funds: These are shares in a fund that owns stock in many companies and is professionally managed.

Exchange Traded Funds (ETF): These are securities that track an index but trade like a stock. They usually have low fees and are considered tax efficient.

Commodities: Owning futures contracts for wheat, corn, soybeans, cotton, and cattle is a form of commodity investing. This is a high-risk category of investing.

Real Estate: Owning income-producing real estate directly or shares in a publicly traded real estate investment trust (REIT) provides current income plus potential for increased value based on changing market values of real estate.

Art: Quality art by proven or rising artists can become more valuable over time. I am not a good reference on the art market.

Precious Metal: Owning gold, silver, and other highly valued metal is a form of investing. These products do not pay interest or dividends and require storage fees and other costs to buy and sell. I do not recommend precious metals for your portfolio.

This list includes only a few products. With each of these investment products, there is a risk of loss in value. Investment funds are always subject to risk, but they can improve the potential returns.

Strategy #5: Combine savings with investments.

Saving a portion of my income on a regular basis has been the foundation on which I have built an investment portfolio. The simple key to adequate retirement income is savings. To have funds for savings, you must be able to live on less than you make. Put another way, your monthly expenses must be less than your income. Start saving early and never stop.

Saving 15 percent of your annual income is what I recommend. For years, I thought building up a savings account and certificates of deposit was how I would fund my future retirement. Times change, and the low rate of return on these safe accounts pushed me into taking more risks and into investing. I know how hard it is to earn a living and provide for all the wants and needs of a young, growing family. I wanted investments that worked as hard for me as I worked to earn the money. Rather than trying to hit a home run (a large profit from sudden share price appreciation) with each investment, my approach has always been to be a slow, steady investor looking to match market returns, year after year.

Strategy #6: Put compound interest to work for you.

I learned about the power of compound interest from high school and college courses, but I never really appreciated how it worked. Putting compound interest to work in the real world made me understand why Albert Einstein called compound interest "the eighth wonder of the world." The simple key to being able to generate adequate retirement income is to start saving early and never stop, letting the power of compound interest build account balances over time.

This concept is so important that I will repeat the strategy. The single, most important tool in building a retirement fund is the power of compound interest. Compound interest is earning interest on top of interest or money earning more money. The periodic interest payments are added to the original principal amount, and in the next time period, the interest is calculated on the expanded amount.

The power of compound interest can work for all age groups. Compound interest can allow an average investor to become wealthy over time. Don't confuse what you need to have accumulated for retirement with what you need to save before retirement. It is all about when you start saving and investing rather than the amount invested. You need to provide savings so compounding can work. Compound interest cannot do all the heavy lifting, but it can help you achieve your long-term financial goals.

Here are a few examples of compound interest at work:

- Save $100 per month for twenty years = $24,000; with compound interest, the total becomes $59,770 (assumes tax-deferred savings at 8 percent).
- Invest in a DRIP Plan (dividend-reinvestment plan) like ConocoPhillips (COP) or McDonald's (MCD); each quarterly dividend adds to the number of shares owned in the company, and the dividends increase because of the additional shares purchased.
- Start a monthly payroll deduction to fund a 401(k) plan or other retirement account where you work. Each monthly investment builds on the previous amount invested plus any interest or dividends earned.

Each of these examples illustrates putting money to work on a regular basis. Each deposit builds on the previous amount—plus what it has earned—and the pool of funds compounds over time.

Tools

There are many online calculators to use for computing compound interest and determining the amount of money accumulated after years of investing. I like the compound interest calculator found at this free website: www.moneychimp.com /compound_interest_calculator.htm.

A second tool is the frequency of compounding or how many times compounding occurs in a twelve-month period. The more frequently money compounds, the faster money grows. Accounts that compound monthly will grow faster and larger than accounts that compound annually. When looking at alternative deposit accounts, ask about the frequency of compounding. It can make a difference.

Strategy #7: The Rule of 72

Another tool to help you measure progress in retirement planning is the Rule of 72. This mathematical formula is simple, and it is helpful in estimating how many years it will take a sum of money invested at a given rate of interest to double. The formula: 72 divided by the interest rate will equal the number of years required to double the investment. For example, 72/5.0 percent = 14.4 years for the sum invested to double earning an interest rate of 5.0 percent. If your initial investment is $10,000 at 5 percent interest, the original amount will double to $20,000 in 14.4 years. Why is this an important tool in retirement planning?

Many people are intimidated by the idea they need to accumulate large amounts of savings to retire comfortably. Because the numbers seem large and unattainable, they give up on saving for retirement before they really get started. Your focus should be on what you need to save currently, not the end amount. This tool will help you estimate how long it will take to accumulate a specific dollar amount for retirement. For example, if your goal is to accumulate a $500,000 nest egg for retirement and you begin saving for this at age thirty-five, you need to save $341 per month, invested at 8.0 percent to have $501,000 at age sixty-five. Interest rates earned and years before retirement are the two biggest variables. Reducing the interest rates and/or extending the time until retirement will generate a different nest egg amount.

Most financial advisers suggest saving 15 percent of gross income annually. If this is too high a percentage, start smaller, but get started. Save and hold is an approach that will keep your savings earning a return. You can always take out a loan for a car, a home, or a college education, but you cannot take out a loan for retirement.

Strategy #8: Determine how much is enough in retirement.

In addition to the Rule of 72, there are other methods of determining the dollar amount needed in retirement. A recent study suggested it may take twenty-two times the annual income you want in retirement to be financially independent. This seems high to me, but it is worth considering. For example, if you want an annual income of $100,000 in retirement (not counting social security), then the total amount to be accumulated in all retirement accounts is $2,200,000 (100,000 x 22 = 2,200,000).

It is important to determine how much is enough in retirement because that is the only way to be able to set a specific dollar goal and work toward achieving that amount. To say you want as much money as possible for retirement is both irrelevant and irresponsible. Many financial planners recommend a target retirement income of 85–100 percent of your preretirement income to sustain the same standard of living you enjoyed prior to retirement. So if you earned $80,000 annually prior to retirement, under this formula, you should consider replacing at least 85 percent of that salary or $68,000 in retirement.

By using either the Rule of 72 or the twenty-two-times-the-anticipated-income approach, you have a way to estimate your progress toward achieving your financial goals. These are tools to help you achieve financial independence.

Strategy #9: Retirement planning is more than just about money.

There is more involved in retirement planning than just the financial strategies to achieve a lifetime of financial independence. This type of planning has more than one dimension. Financial planning receives the majority of attention and discussion and is the focus of this book, but other factors should be considered that are of equal or greater importance. Some call this broader approach to retirement planning *life planning*. Where do you want to live in retirement, and what is the cost of living in that location? How will you occupy your time? Do you want to stay involved in business, do volunteer work, or both? Will you be able to travel and spend time with family and friends? What about health issues and health care planning? Are there family members in need of support or your services as a caregiver? These and other issues require you to think ahead and plan for the future. You should develop your personal plans to address these questions before retirement. Each person has a different set of priorities in retirement. What are yours?

Now that you have the basic strategies outlined above, let's turn to addressing some of the more significant life issues you will need to resolve.

Chapter 2

Employment

This is your first priority after graduating from college! Make finding a job your full-time activity. In other words, make finding a full-time job your job. Conduct numerous interviews and learn from each one. Make your selection from the best options available. Be willing to start at a low level and work your way up. It all starts with getting a job.

Rules for Success

I hope you will find a job doing something you really enjoy. Follow my six rules for success, and you will be off to a very good start in building a career.

- Show up on time, ready to work every day.
- Dress for success. Dress for the position you want. Avoid being too casual.
- Be an enthusiastic student of the business. Learn and read what you can about the industry. Sign up for course work to become outstanding in your field. Work with your industry trade association to broaden your knowledge and contacts.

- Be involved daily. Do not just go through the motions, waiting for the time to go home. Return all phone calls and e-mails the same day you receive them. Learn to be responsive.
- Take on special projects and team activities to raise your visibility within the company.
- Always be networking. Develop the skills to be a business producer. Every company needs employees who can grow the business with new accounts, new product ideas, and new or different services.

These rules are not difficult to follow. It just takes daily effort to stay focused on producing tangible results for your employer in return for a paycheck. The better you apply these simple rules, the more valuable you become to your employer. This is the definition of job security. Just remember: you get hired for your skills, but you get fired for your behavior.

Employment is not a lifetime commitment to one company. It can be, but reality proves most people have multiple jobs throughout their careers. One of my mentors was fond of saying, "A career is a series of different job assignments."

Careers are built on experience. Enter the workforce with an attitude of being willing to learn. Starting with an entry-level job may be the first step. Look for opportunities to move up in responsibility and salary within the same company. When you feel you have reached a plateau and cannot move higher because of corporate culture, glass ceiling, age of your supervisor, problems in the economy, or corporate downsizing, consider moving to another company that will value your experience and offer an upward career trajectory.

Chapter 3

Budgeting

My simple philosophy for building a retirement fund is to live on less than you make, invest the balance carefully, and be patient. Let compound interest work for you while you enjoy spending time with family and friends and pursuing your career. To be able to successfully save and invest, you must create a budget. Knowing where you spend money is the first step to understanding how much will be available for saving or investing.

Budget steps

- List monthly net income (after taxes and all other deductions): $3,000.
- Deduct fixed expenses such as rent, mortgage payments, utilities, food, and child care: $1,800.
- After subtracting expenses from net income, this is your discretionary fund: $1,200.
- Deduct a savings amount of 15 percent of net pay: $450.
- What is left is what you have to spend for entertainment, going out to dinner, and other luxuries. This results in $750 per month discretionary fund after savings.

Are you a spender or a saver? One of the first steps in deciding how much you can save each month is to prepare a budget and track monthly income and expenses. People tend to put off budgeting for the same reasons they don't start an exercise program or go on a diet. They feel they just don't have the time commitment or know how to get started.

The Benefits of Budgeting

Budgeting gives you a chance to set priorities and make deliberate choices about where to spend money and how much to save. Keep budgeting simple. Figure out where you are now financially. List your fixed expenses like mortgage payments, rent, utility bills, child care, and food. Subtract those expenses from your net pay. This will let you know how much you have left for savings and discretionary spending. Next, do what works for you. Use a manual system or one of the many online spreadsheets. You need to know where your money is being spent each month.

Monitor your progress over time. It will help keep you on target. You may find you can increase your savings amount with very little effort. At a minimum, budgeting should give you the peace of mind that you are in charge of your spending and savings.

Some people make budgeting too complicated by entering every expenditure down to the penny. Others take a more global view and only track expenses above twenty-five dollars. Both concepts can be effective. Use a method that works for you. If you do not know where you spend money, you will not know how much is available to save or where you can reduce some of your expenses. Budgeting is all about you—no one else.

Chapter 4

Pay Yourself First

Strategy #10: Make paying yourself first a lifelong commitment.

This is a concept foreign to many working people who are living paycheck to paycheck. Save something out of every month's income. Build a cash reserve equal to three to six months of expenses. This will give you a cushion for all the unplanned events that always occur. I recommend a goal of saving one hundred dollars per month to start. This is called paying yourself first because you put away the hundred dollars before you do anything else with your paycheck.

I recommend putting these funds into a savings account for up to three months of emergency expenses and depositing additional savings into a Roth IRA. Remember—the principal in a Roth IRA can be withdrawn after five years and age fifty-nine and a half without penalty and tax-free. The funds in a Roth IRA have the potential for higher returns than a savings account. There is more information about IRAs in a later chapter. If you cannot wait until age fifty-nine and a half, just keep adding to your savings account up to six months of expenses.

General Rules for Saving and Borrowing

Try to pay cash for most purchases. If you use a credit card with attractive reward points or miles, then pay off the balance in full each month. Major purchases like autos or a home may require some type of financing. When you do finance a purchase, try to pay it off quickly. Why pay all that interest to someone else? Use an automatic payroll deduction for the amount to save when you get started. If you never see the money, it is easier to live without it. Having the highest salary is not the preferred measurement. How much you keep at the end of the month, after taxes, is what really counts. Putting money aside for retirement is a priority. To bet on a different outcome would take a triumph of hope over experience.

If you have the discipline to pay off credit card balances in full each month, this can be another way to pay for everyday expenses. Many credit card companies offer incentives for usage such as airline miles, discounts on major purchases, or an annual cash-back program. I even buy groceries with a credit card to earn mileage points. If any of these are important to you, I encourage you to explore the many options available. The key is to be able to pay off the full balance each month.

Chapter 5

Good Debt versus Bad Debt

All debt is not created equal. Know good debt from bad. If the interest on the debt is not tax deductible, then it is bad debt. Borrowing to increase long-term wealth or security, such as an education or a home, is an investment in the future. Borrowing to buy something that decreases in value (depreciates), like consumer goods, autos, or mobile devices, creates extra expenses because they will need to be replaced. Credit card debt, automobile debt, and other types of installment debt will only prevent you from saving enough and achieving your goal of a lifetime of financial independence.

Home Mortgage Debt

A home mortgage is good debt, and a thirty-year fixed-interest rate provides the lowest payment options. Make sure there are no prepayment penalties since you may want to double up on payments to lessen the mortgage term to fifteen years by making two payments a month instead of one. The Internal Revenue Service allows interest paid on a mortgage to be tax deductible, and this encourages home ownership over renting. The less interest you pay someone else, the more you have for saving and investing for your future. Most home mortgages require a minimum of 20 percent cash down payment because lenders prefer to loan no more than 80 percent of the appraised value of the home. This down payment requirement is called having skin in the game.

Beware of marketing promotions from retailers that offer no interest for ninety days or 0 percent interest for five years; these are come-ons to get you to buy their products. These programs factor in the cost of no financing in the price of the product. There are no free lunches when it comes to debt. However, sometimes to satisfy individual wants or needs, debt may make sense. Just know the difference between good and bad debt and be aware of the consequences.

Strategy #11: Be smart about how you handle debt.

Set priorities for savings versus paying down debt. Is there ever a time when saving for retirement may not be your first priority? Yes. One example is the need to pay off high-interest-rate credit card balances. Eliminating these debts may take precedence over savings. Interest on these types of debt is not tax deductible. If you do not have high-interest credit card debt, after making a contribution to your retirement plan, go after reducing other types of debt.

Chapter 6

Invest on a Regular Basis

The first rule of investing is not to lose money.
The second rule is not to forget the first rule.
—Warren Buffett

Key Definitions

Dollar-Cost Averaging: By investing a small sum of money over time, you will ultimately own more shares with varying prices than if one amount was invested all at once. This is considered a conservative method of investing.

No-Load Funds: These mutual funds and index funds have no up-front fees to purchase them. No-load funds have no commissions or fees.

Index Funds: This is a type of mutual fund that buys all the stocks in a specific index, such as the S&P 500. The investment results should equate to the return on the index (less any fees).

Passive Fund Investing: The best example is an index fund; the fund manager is not trying to select investments that will exceed the index return; passive management is investing made easy.

Begin investing on a regular basis—monthly, quarterly, or semiannually—and stay with your plan. True investors avoid the negatives of buying fads or the latest recommendations from a broker, highly leveraged companies, or trying to time the market (sometimes called momentum investing). Markets reward patience more than any other skill.

Strategy #12: Mutual funds are a good product for beginning investors.

Mutual funds might be a good place to start. These funds are professionally managed, collective pools of investable funds that combine money from many different investors to purchase securities. When you invest in a mutual fund, you own shares in the fund—not shares in the individual companies that comprise the fund. At last count, there were more than 7,500 funds available, and that number is growing. This is too many funds to evaluate in total.

Index Funds

A special type of mutual fund is an index fund. A good way to start investing and learning about the process is by starting with a low-cost index fund instead of picking individual stocks. Consider putting money in over time to take advantage of dollar-cost averaging. To achieve good returns at a reasonable risk level, index funds provide several benefits in one solution.

Benefits of Index Funds

- Offers diversification of investments.
- Don't try to beat the market or index—just equal the performance of the benchmark.
- Don't try to time the market.
- Invest in small amounts on a regular basis.
- Keep investment expenses low.
- Provide professional management.

Buying a broad index fund over time can be a cornerstone of building an investment portfolio. You might consider funds like Vanguard Total Stock Market Index (VTSKMKT), Vanguard 500 Index Fund (VFINX), or Fidelity Growth Company Fund (FDGRX). Index fund investing is considered boring by some because your investment is tracking an index of stocks. Boring is good when it comes to investing in index funds.

There are many mutual fund company choices. Several of my favorites are T. Rowe Price, Fidelity Investments, and Vanguard. All three have no-load funds and small initial investment requirements. These are good choices because they have low expenses, good historical performance track records, and experienced fund managers. The individual fund manager does make a difference. Make sure he or she has experience managing that particular fund and check out past performance as measured by annual returns compared with the benchmark. You always want managers who have met or exceeded the benchmark over time.

Passively Managed Funds

Vanguard is one of the lowest-cost mutual fund companies. Their expenses are low, and they charge no up-front fees. They pioneered the concept of an index fund: a basket of investments that match the selected benchmark, such as the S&P 500, the Total Market, Largest 100 Companies, etc. If you choose to invest in a Vanguard Index Fund, pick an index that has broad market representation. Investing this way will let you match that particular market's annual performance. These are called passively managed funds.

Strategy #13: Avoid hedge funds and actively managed accounts.

I do not recommend individual investments in hedge funds, separately managed accounts, or other types of alternative investment products for individual investors. Many of these are labeled actively managed accounts. These are for professional investors and require larger initial investment amounts than passively managed accounts. Actively managed accounts also have higher fees. Stay away from hedge funds and actively managed accounts.

Strategy #14: Use dollar-cost averaging.

Investing periodically, over time, is preferable to dropping a large sum into any of these funds. This allows you to get the positive effect of dollar-cost averaging. Using dollar-cost averaging allows you to buy shares in the fund over time, thereby averaging fund prices. By investing the same dollar amount each time, you buy more shares when prices are low and fewer shares when prices are higher. Usually this method of investing will allow you to acquire more shares at a more favorable price than lump-sum investing.

Strategy #15: Develop financial discipline.

Begin investing periodically—and stick with it. This is half of the definition of financial discipline; the other half of the definition is leaving the funds fully invested and not withdrawing any funds other than for a real emergency. In my experience, lack of financial discipline is one of the most frequent reasons people do not achieve financial independence in retirement.

Out-of-control impulse buying or wanting a new auto every year are examples of how people lose their saving and investing discipline during the financial accumulation years before retirement. Exercise some personal restraint when it comes to wanting every new model cell phone or mobile device the week they become available. The benefits from this self-restraint will be enjoyed in many years of retirement financial security.

Chapter 7

Bonds and Other Fixed-Income Investments

Key Definitions

Fixed Income: As a term, fixed income is interchangeable with a bond—any investment that pays a fixed amount of interest on a regular basis.

Safe-Haven Investment: This type of investment is considered safe from market volatility or dramatic swings in price or return. United States government bonds are one type of safe haven investment.

Rated Bonds: These bonds have been rated for financial quality by a rating agency like Fitch, S&P, or Moody's. The bond issuer pays to obtain the rating; rated bonds are considered more secure and liquid than unrated bonds. Bond investing is like listening to the rhythm of the rain. Slow and steady, yet the rain brings an annual rebirth of nature. Bonds too can add life to an investment portfolio.

As a general rule, recessions are bad for equities and good for bonds. Bonds are debt instruments of corporations, municipalities, and the federal government. Bonds are considered a primary form of fixed-income investment products. They are thought of as a safe haven (safe from loss in value if held to maturity) investment that pays a fixed rate of interest semiannually and returns 100 percent of the principal at maturity. However, there are risks: increasing interest rates push the prices for bonds down, there are inflation risks with any fixed-payment investment, market risks like corporate bankruptcy and financial restructuring, municipal insolvency, and default.

As a bond investor, your total return is the sum of any price changes in the bond plus the interest income.

Corporate bonds can be investment grade, rated, nonrated, or junk bonds. Just remember: the higher the yield, the higher the potential risk.

Are individual bonds better than bond funds? Unless you are investing larger sums of money, bond funds are usually a better deal. Make sure to watch the expenses of the fund. If you are paying more than 0.5 percent in annual fees, you may be overpaying. Individual bonds usually come in $25,000 denominations, but investments in bond funds can be for smaller amounts.

Strategy #16: Avoid bonds until around age fifty.

The time for taking risk in investing is when you are young and have many years to recover from any mistakes or bad investments. I chose to be 100 percent invested in large-cap growth stocks until I was fifty. At that age, I realized it was time to develop a more conservative investment philosophy since my number of years before retirement was shrinking quickly. I began to diversify into selected dividend-paying stocks and a few bonds. John Bogel, founder and inventor of index funds for Vanguard, believes a bond portfolio percentage of a total investment portfolio should equal your age. For example, at age sixty, you should have 60 percent fixed income and 40 percent stocks. At age seventy, you should have 70 percent fixed income and 30 percent stock. This is a very conservative investment strategy. I think you need to continue to own at least 60 percent equities throughout your lifetime to protect against inflation risk. Entering retirement with a 60 percent equity and 40 percent bond portfolio has met my expectations for achieving financial independence.

Chapter 8

Individual Stock Selection

Key Definitions

Capital Appreciation: This is the increase in the price of the investment.

DRIP (Dividend Reinvestment Plan): Some major companies offer this service to shareholders. Instead of paying dividends to the shareholder in cash, the company uses the dividend to buy more stock in the same company. This is an advantageous way to accumulate stock in a company.

Active Trading: This professional, computer-driven method of rapid buy/sell orders for stocks is not for ordinary investors.

Total Return: This is the sum of income plus the price appreciation of the investment.

Price-to-Book Ratio: This is a formula of the stock price divided by the book value. An amount above 1:00 indicates the price is a premium above book value.

Price-Earnings Ratio: This is a formula of the stock price divided by the earnings per share (EPS) of the stock. The resulting answer indicates how many times the stock price is compared to the share EPS (a higher number means more premium for the earnings).

Phantom Income: This is income from an investment you never see, hold, or receive because it is being automatically reinvested in stock of the company. A DRIP is an example of phantom income.

Strategy #17: Do-It-Yourself investing is cost efficient

Beware of people selling financial products for a commission! As the saying goes, "Never ask a barber if you need a haircut." The answer is predictable. Likewise, never ask a commissioned broker whether buying or selling a stock is a good idea. As a do-it-yourself (DIY) investor, opening an account with one of the online brokerage firms may be a good choice. I recommend using an online brokerage account such as Fidelity, TD Ameritrade, E-Trade, or Schwab for equity research as well as buying, selling, and holding equities. These accounts are easy to open, have a low initial investment threshold, and charge low fees.

Don't believe for a minute that you can compete with the computer-driven, rapid-fire trading systems used by some brokerage firms. Active trading is for professionals, and so is day trading. Avoid these investing strategies. The market rewards patience over all other investing skills.

Strategy #18: Good companies perform well over time with a buy-and-hold strategy.

As a casual investor, select good companies with a track record of solid earnings and a history of increasing dividends. After all, a buy-and-hold strategy will reward you with a collect-and-win result. Either collect the dividends in direct payments to you or set up a DRIP (dividend reinvestment program) with those companies that offer such an option. Letting dividends be automatically reinvested in more stock is one way to accumulate a sizable stock ownership position in a few companies. DRIP reinvestments are still taxable in the year in which the dividends are paid. This is like paying taxes on phantom income because you never see the cash, but you do receive increasing stock ownership.

Strategy #19: Put some investments on autopilot.

I bought my first stock when I was in high school. It was Phillips 66, which is now known as ConocoPhillips (COP). They offered a DRIP plan, and I have been in that plan for many years. Through market highs and lows, I bought COP stock automatically every quarter with the dividends. This is like having an investment on autopilot. COP has continued to perform well and increase their dividends on a regular basis. I still own COP today.

Strategy #20: Enjoy the benefits of owning dividend-paying stocks.

Why do I like dividend-paying stocks? Dividend-paying stocks are appealing for four reasons. First, since 1926, dividends have accounted for almost 42 percent of the total return of the S&P 500. Second, federal taxes on dividends have been favorable. Currently, dividend tax rates are 20 percent on dividends versus a higher rate for ordinary income. Third, dividend-paying companies offer a source of cash flow to shareholders through quarterly payments. This will generate additional funds for living expenses or investing. Finally, dividend-paying companies tend to be more stable and demonstrate a stronger return to shareholders through their dividend and stock buyback programs.

Strategy #21: Value stocks are the core of my portfolio.

Many dividend-paying stocks are in the style category of value stocks. Value stocks are defined as stocks that trade for less than their intrinsic value. There is no exact definition of intrinsic value for a stock; it is an estimate of the true value of a company based on financial strength, brand recognition, and market share criteria.

Some people define value stocks as those selling for less than book value. Book value per share for a company is determined by total assets minus total liability equals net worth. Net worth divided by the total number of shares outstanding will equal book value per share. Usually, value investors select stocks with lower than average price-to-book or price-to-earnings ratios. This is the classic definition of buying a stock for less than what it is really worth. Another way of describing value stocks is that value stocks are inexpensive relative to their earnings, and they tend to outperform more expensive stocks over time. Most value stocks have low price-to-earnings ratios.

Some of the most famous value investors of my time have been Benjamin Graham, David Dodd, and Warren Buffett. In 2014, Warren Buffett named his top ten value stocks. Some of the names may surprise you. These are listed in order of his largest amount invested in each one:

- Wells Fargo (WFC)—commercial banking and financial services
- Coca-Cola (KO)—consumer products
- American Express (AXP)—financial services and credit cards
- International Business Machines (IBM)—information technology

- Procter and Gamble (PG)—large number of consumer products
- ExxonMobil (XOM)—international energy company
- Walmart (WMT)—world's largest retailer
- US Bancorp (USB)—commercial banking and financial services
- DirecTV (DTV)—subscriber service to consumers
- DaVita Healthcare Partners (DVA)—health care

Strategy #22: Invest for total return.

Another investment strategy compared to just measuring dividend yield is called a *total return strategy*. This is an approach in buying stocks that have both dividends and capital appreciation. An example is Procter and Gamble, which has increased dividends for more than four decades. The total return accounts for both income and capital appreciation. Capital appreciation represents the change in the market price of a stock from the time of purchase to date of sale.

Strategy #23: Develop a buy strategy and a sell strategy.

All investors need a buy strategy *and* a sell strategy. The classic combination of strategies is to buy low and sell high. Knowing when to sell will help avoid holding a stock or mutual fund too long. As markets change, various industries go in and out of favor. Selling a stock in an industry that has lost favor with the market, like coal mining or ethanol plants, can free up funds for investments in more growth industries.

Long-term investing means more than owning the investment for more than twelve months. It also means holding investments as long as they are doing well and meeting your original goal for owning them. Annually, ask yourself if—given all you know about the company or fund—would you buy it at today's price? If not, consider selling it. If a fund manager departs, it could be a signal to sell. Long-term investing also has a tax consequence: holding a stock for at least twelve months qualifies any profit from the sale to be taxed at a lower rate known as the capital gains rate. Long-term capital gains tax rates are lower than tax rates on short-term gains. Short-term gains are taxed as ordinary income.

Watch asset bloat, meaning when a fund grows so large it becomes too cumbersome to manage efficiently. Performance below the market index is another reason to sell a fund and move on. Tax consequences of selling should be considered, whether a loss or a profit, but this should not be the only reason for selling. These strategies are of less value if you are only investing in passively managed index funds. In this case, you are only trying to match the market index.

Strategy #24: Keep investment expenses low.

Control one of the few things you can control in investing by watching expenses and costs. The lower the expense, the better. The less you pay in fees, the more you have to invest. Investing in index funds is one of the purest forms of low-cost investing. Index funds have some of the lowest expenses. Expenses include commissions to buy or sell, management fees, marketing fees, and any other fees paid by the investor. The less paid in expenses, the more realized in returns.

Strategy #25: Keep it simple.

Keep your investing strategy simple; if you want to earn good returns at a reasonable risk level, follow a careful selection of individual, dividend-paying stocks. Twenty to twenty-five different stocks will be more than enough to track. If you prefer to have some or all of your investments in index funds, this market matching strategy will work too.

Avoid more exotic market moves using options, puts, and calls. Don't try to time the market or become a day trader; those strategies turn investing into nothing more than gambling. Time in the market remains the best way to build a solid investment portfolio. You are building a retirement fund to last a lifetime—not running an investment sprint to win the performance-of-the-month award. Ultimately, time is the most valuable, nonrenewable resource available to investors.

Strategy #26: Buy shares in the company where you work.

It is a common aspiration for employees to want to own shares of stock in the company where they work. This is possible if you work for a publicly traded company, but is it a good investment decision?

Owning shares in your employer is a good thing. It helps align your investment interests with the financial performance of the company. You will share in the increased value of the company as reflected in an increasing price of the shares. This is a positive correlation between the hard work of all employees and an increased value of shares in your employer.

How can employees buy shares in their employers? There are several ways to invest in the shares of your employer:

1. Stock options may be granted as part of an incentive plan.
2. Restrictive stock may be issued for time-in-service awards or promotions.
3. The 401(k) company match may be in company stock (watch the vesting schedule).
4. Purchases of stock can be made on the open market.

Any one or all these ownership options can be beneficial to your portfolio.

Several questions arise with employer stock ownership. How much stock should you own? Is there a limit? How much is too much? Why should you have a concern about how many shares you own of your employer?

Your employer represents the primary source of income for you and your family. If these paychecks stop for any reason (layoffs, downsizing, financial difficulties, pay cuts), how would you continue to provide for your family? If any of these situations were to occur, you would be hard-pressed to sustain your current standard of living. I would not compound this potential problem by owning a large percentage of my investment portfolio in my employer's stock.

Diversification of investments by company and industry remains an important decision for you. My rule of thumb for owning stock in your employer is to limit that ownership to no more than 10–15 percent of your total investment portfolio.

Another way to limit ownership might be to set a maximum dollar exposure—say $100,000. For example, if you have a total portfolio of $500,000, limit your employer's shares to no more than $75,000 in face value from all sources of stock ownership. This same rule of thumb can be applied to any company in your portfolio to avoid overconcentration. Stay diversified by spreading the investment risks. This is particularly important when it comes to share ownership in your employer.

Chapter 9

Diversify and Rebalance

Key Definitions

Allocation: Investing your portfolio in different asset classes (stocks, bonds, money market accounts, or commodities). A typical example might be 80 percent equities and 20 percent fixed income.

Diversify: Purchase different securities in different industries (domestic and international).

Rebalance: Maintain your asset allocation over time. At least annually, sell some of your best performers and buy more of the lesser-performing asset classes to maintain your planned allocation (for example, 80 percent equities and 20 percent fixed income). After a rise in stock prices, you might find your year-end allocation at 90–10; if so, sell some of the stocks and buy more fixed income.

Correlation: Correlation coefficients measure the level by which one security tracks another security. These coefficients range from –1 to +1 (a correlation coefficient of –1 implies that a security increases in price every time the market decreases in price). Even with low correlations, these investments should be evaluated for value and return potential. Correlation coefficients can be found in most equity research publications.

Beta: This is a measure of the volatility of an individual security in comparison to the entire market. Beta of less than 1.0 means the security is less volatile, and greater than 1.0 is considered more volatile than the market. Beta is a general measure of risk.

Strategy #27: Pay attention to asset allocation.

You don't have to be a longtime student of the stock market to be a successful investor. You can't control the economy, market direction, or the past performance of index funds or individual stocks. Neither can anyone else. What you can control is how you allocate your investments. This involves how you spread your investable funds among individual stocks, index funds, bonds, and short-term investments like money market funds (MMF).

Invest to stay ahead of inflation. The effects of inflation risk increase over time because inflation reduces your buying power. A 4 percent annual inflation rate can reduce the purchasing power of $1,000 down to $456 in twenty years. This is why putting a high percentage of your investment portfolio in safe investments like MMF can increase risk over time.

Cash can be one of the most risky investment categories when it comes to mitigating inflation risk. Having large cash balances can also cause you to suffer missed opportunity costs while staying only in cash. While you will have large cash balances available, you will suffer investor anxiety over missing many opportunities in the market to buy at lower prices. I believe in staying fully invested.

A portfolio that is diversified between equities, bonds, and MMF should reduce both market risk and inflation risk. What is the appropriate amount in each category? It depends on your age, your risk tolerance, and your total investable assets.

The goal of asset allocation is combining different asset types that complement each other to maximize potential returns and reduce risk. Some call this looking for a low correlation among and between asset classes. I call it smart investing!

Some important factors to consider include your time horizon until retirement and your personal risk profile. In general, if you have many years before retirement and a higher risk tolerance, more emphasis on equities might be appropriate. Investing 100 percent in equities may be appropriate until age fifty or so. If you have a shorter time horizon to retirement and a lower risk tolerance, more fixed income and MMF make sense. Being invested in stocks and/or index funds will always give you more inflation risk coverage than fixed-income investments.

Asset allocation should be reviewed regularly. It is not a cumbersome procedure, and it may make a meaningful difference in total investment performance. Follow these steps:

- Use quarterly or year-end statements to review existing allocations.
- Calculate the current percentage mix of equities, fixed income, and cash equivalents.
- Make investment decisions to bring the allocation back into your desired formula (for example, 60 percent equity and 40 percent fixed income with some variable for cash).
- Execute on your decisions and put the statements away until the end of the next quarter.

Chapter 10

IRA (Individual Retirement Accounts) and 401(k) Accounts

Key Definitions

Disciplined Investor: Have a plan of action and consistently follow through with the plan.

Autopilot Investing: A DRIP investment is an example of investing without taking any action. Another example is a monthly payroll deduction for savings.

Tax-Deferred Investing: This is one of the most tax-advantageous forms of investing because all taxes due on earned income in this form of investment are deferred until the funds are withdrawn. Always try to maximize this type of investing.

Strategy #28: Overcome inertia.

Time in the market is much more important than timing the market. This is especially true when investing for retirement. To achieve any goal, an individual must find a way to harness one of the most powerful forces in the universe: *inertia*. Having no plan, doing nothing for your future retirement security, and living from paycheck to paycheck is a common form of financial inertia.

My approach to overcome inertia in financial planning for retirement has been to become a disciplined investor. What is a disciplined investor? A disciplined investor is one who sets targets or financial goals for things that are personally important and then devises a plan to achieve them. One example might be saving for a new car. If the car costs $24,000, how much should you save monthly to buy the car? Over a five-year period, saving $400 per month (400 x 60 months = 24,000) will provide enough to buy the car.

If you receive periodic gifts of money for your birthday or Christmas, these lump sums added to the savings account could decrease the required monthly amount. Saving for a down payment on a house, vacation, college funds, or retirement are other examples of financial goals.

Once you have decided on a goal, you need to maintain the financial discipline to make the monthly deposits to achieve those goals. If you want help making periodic deposits, you can establish payroll deductions with your employer to set aside the funds before you receive your paycheck. Money market accounts that pay interest are a good, safe place to accumulate these savings. Other examples of the automatic approach might be enrolling in your company's 401(k) plan or creating an annual increase to your savings rate by 1 percent per year. If you are self-employed, then creating a self-directed individual 401(k) plan with monthly investments from a MMF would be an example.

Strategy #29: Maximize tax-deferred investment opportunities.

Always look for ways to maximize tax-deferred savings and investments. Many employers offer 401(k), 403(b), or Section 457 plans. There are tax-deferred retirement plan options for the self-employed, as well as IRA, SEP-IRA, profit-sharing plans, and self-directed 401(k) plans. Protect the tax-deferral status of these investments when you change jobs. You can maintain this status by rolling over the plan balances into another plan like an IRA. You must follow strict guidelines to avoid any penalties in these rollovers. Be sure not to overlook these rollover rules.

The time to think seriously about your retirement is when you start your first full-time job. For most twenty-five-year olds, the idea of retirement is not at the top of their minds. It should be because saving even a small amount early can make a difference. A twenty-five-year-old who starts saving just $600 a year would have $72,000 at age sixty-five, which is nearly twice as much as someone who saves $1,200 a year beginning at age forty-five. The difference is the power of compound interest.

Strategy #30: The two most important accounts for building retirement security are individual retirement accounts (IRA) and 401(k) accounts.

If I had to make only *one* recommendation for securing your financial independence, it would be to encourage you to make regular contributions to *both* an IRA and a 401(k) account. I prefer funding a Roth IRA annually to the maximum because this type of IRA offers a combination of tax-deferred earnings *and* tax-free withdrawals. If you do not qualify because of the annual income limitations for a Roth, then use a regular IRA account. It still offers tax-deferred earnings, but withdrawals will be taxed as ordinary income.

Most employers offer a 401(k) plan as part of their total benefits package. These retirement savings accounts are part of defined contribution pension plans that have replaced traditional pension plans. Many companies offer a match when you participate in their plans. Sometimes this match can be 3–6 percent of your salary.

At a minimum, your contribution should be at least an amount equal to the company match. For example, if your annual gross salary is $50,000 and your employer offers a 3 percent match, at the end of the year, your employer will deposit $1,500 into your 401(k) account (assuming you are making a contribution equal to this match amount or more). This company match is one of the only sources of free money.

The vesting schedule for a company-sponsored 401(k) plan is also important. Vesting is a term that defines what percentage of the company match an employee owns over time. This schedule outlines the vesting percentage in the company match for each year of employment. Some companies have vesting schedules that increase the vesting percentage annually by 20 percent; at the end of five years of employment, you own the entire company match deposited in your 401(k) account. If you leave the company employment before the five-year limit, you will forfeit a percentage of the company match in accordance with the vesting schedule. Be sure you understand the vesting schedule so you do not forfeit these matching funds prematurely.

Both IRAs and 401(k) plans have a maximum limit that can be contributed annually by you. The company match does not count against the limit. These limits can change from year to year. For 2016, these maximum contribution limits were:

- IRA: $5,500 plus a $1,000 catch-up limit for people age fifty or older
- 401(k): $18,000 with a $6,000 catch-up limit for people age fifty or older

The two most important accounts for successful retirement planning are IRA and 401(k) accounts. You should have both. Anyone with earned income can have an IRA account. Whether it is tax-deductible or not, the IRA is a good tool for tax-deferred investing. Spouses are eligible for IRAs (whether they have earned income or not) with the same limitations on contributions.

Let your IRA build in value over time. Never withdraw funds from your IRA unless it is for a real emergency. If you withdraw funds (other than for an emergency) before age fifty-nine and a half, the penalties are severe. You may be required to take a minimum distribution annually (RMD) from a regular IRA starting at age seventy and a half. These RMD amounts are calculated based on an IRS mortality table that changes annually with your age.

Prioritize withdrawals from different accounts.

Upon retirement, prioritizing withdrawals and other distributions from retirement accounts should be done with tax efficiency in mind. The idea is to initially withdraw funds from accounts that are taxable and leave funds invested in tax-deferred accounts for as long as possible. An exception to this approach might be in early retirement when it is assumed you are in a higher tax bracket. Start withdrawals from a Roth IRA because they are tax-free. In a few years, switch to withdrawals from taxable accounts (as your tax bracket declines). As a general rule, start withdrawing funds from accounts in the following order:

- *Taxable Accounts:* These earnings are subject to tax; by taking withdrawals, taxes are reduced because the earnings are reduced.
- *Social Security:* This is subject to tax up to 85 percent after retirement until your full retirement age of sixty-seven.
- *Tax-Deferred Accounts (IRA or 401(k) Plans):* These invested funds earn tax-deferred status until they are withdrawn. Leave these funds invested as long as possible.

Regular IRA withdrawals are taxed at the ordinary income tax rate.

- *Roth IRA:* These invested funds earn tax-free status and withdrawals are tax-free since these contributions were made after taxes had been paid, you have owned the account at least five years, and you are age fifty-nine and a half or older. Leave these funds invested as long as possible; there is no required RMD (required minimum distribution).

Sources of Retirement Income

- social security
- pension benefits from company plans or military retirement plans
- IRA and 401(k) plans
- personal investment income (dividends and interest)
- part-time employment or self-employment income

Strategy #31: Be careful about beneficiary designations.

An overlooked detail with IRA and 401(k) accounts is the beneficiary designation. Anytime you make changes in these retirement accounts, make sure to update the beneficiary designation, even if you are not making changes to the beneficiaries. If the account numbers of the IRA or 401(k) account do not match the account numbers on the beneficiary designation form currently on file, the accounts will not flow directly to the designated beneficiary—or there may be delays or different tax implications for the beneficiaries. It is a simple step to ensure these accounts pass along to whomever you want when you want—without complications. See the estate-planning chapter to understand that a written will cannot supersede the beneficiary designation on these two types of retirement accounts.

Review the new myRA account.

President Barrack Obama proposed a new, no-frills retirement account in his State of the Union address in January 2014. This proposed account is called myRA, and it is being designed as a retirement savings account for workers without access to a company-sponsored 401(k) plan. It will operate like a Roth IRA: contributions will be made after-tax and grow tax-free. The account will be available to individuals earning less than $129,000 annually and have a contribution limit of $5,500 each year. These accounts will offer a single investment option: a US savings bond that pays a low rate of interest. The US government will guarantee the principal amount, and each account will be capped at $15,000.

While there are inflation risks associated with this account, it is another way to start saving for retirement. At a minimum, these accounts may offer an attractive rate of return for a short-term savings account. There are no penalties for early withdrawal. I think there are better options available, such as a Roth IRA or a traditional IRA, but this new retirement savings account should be evaluated when all the details are available.

You may choose to include these new accounts as part of your retirement planning process—or not. At this time, there is very little information available to review. I do not know at this publication date when or if this retirement account will be available or modified in some way. At the end of the day, the 2016 annual dollar limit of $5,500 applies to any and all IRAs in your portfolio. Choose the one or combination of different accounts that best meets your individual circumstances.

Chapter 11

Life, Disability, and Long-Term-Care Insurance

Life, disability, and long-term-care insurance (LTC) can be the solution to the triple threat of the risk of untimely death, disability, or serious health issues that can drain your savings.

Strategy #32: Mitigate risks through insurance.

As you assume more responsibility with a growing family, it is time to consider how you will provide for your family in the untimely event of your death, disability, or the need for long-term care.

Life Insurance

Whole life, universal life, and term insurance can be confusing concepts. In very simple terms, there are two primary types of life insurance: term life and permanent life. Term life insurance offers a death benefit during a certain number of years (often twenty years). Permanent life insurance, which includes whole life and universal life policies, is designed to remain in force for the policyholder's entire life. Both term and whole life offer a specific dollar amount death benefit. Whole life buyers usually pay a fixed premium for the life of the policy, which covers all fees, while building up cash value that can be used to purchase additional insurance. In contrast, most universal life buyers pay a flexible premium amount and anticipate using returns on cash value accounts within the policy to pay for future premiums. Premiums are lower the younger you are when you initially purchase life insurance (assuming you are in good health).

Buyers of universal life often do so because they want insurance to last longer than term insurance coverage. Many of these policies have hidden fees and costs. Universal life policies combine a death benefit with a tax-advantaged savings account. Beware the assumptions used in universal policies like interest rates, inflation rates, and rates of return. Most of the time, they are not realistic. For example, they may assume inflation at a very low rate and return on investments at a very high rate. Neither case may be reality. These policies have assumptions about future interest rates and investment returns. If these assumptions are too aggressive and do not match the market, the policyholder will be paying a higher premium than was originally assumed.

Term life insurance is the simplest form of insurance. There are numerous websites to obtain term insurance quotes. Working with a licensed life insurance agent with a CLU designation or going online is your choice. Term insurance may have the lowest cost for the amount of coverage. It provides a specific death benefit for a stated number of years at a fixed annual premium. When the time period covered by the policy expires, the insurance is canceled—and you have nothing to show for the years you paid premiums. It is very straightforward. Term insurance can be important as a way to cover a high-risk period of your life, such as when your children are young and you are still building your net worth through investing. I recommend a combination of term and whole life during the years you have children living at home. Converting whole life policies to single-premium-pay policies when you are an empty nester may be a good use of these life insurance policies later in life.

I have always looked at life insurance as risk mitigation and buying peace of mind. It mitigates the risk of dying early before you can provide other financial security for your family, and it gives you and your family peace of mind that, if an early death were to occur, you have provided financial security to cover this contingency. Life insurance is not a good savings strategy. It does offer tax-deferred cash buildup in cash value, but other savings instruments offer better returns. I have owned all three types of life insurance, and I have used them to cover any outstanding indebtedness upon death as well as for estate-planning purposes.

How much insurance do you need?

How much life insurance is enough? Ask any three life insurance salesmen, and you will get three different answers. The real answer depends on how much you want to leave to your family in the way of financial assets upon your death in combination with how successful you are at living to an old age and being able to accumulate other assets. Some people choose not to leave their families much in life insurance proceeds upon their death, believing that their heirs should earn their own ways in life. Others prefer to leave their families some financial cushion to assist them in the future. These life insurance beneficiaries will still need to work, save, and plan, but they will inherit some funds upon the death of a parent.

I have used life insurance to help me accomplish this goal through detailed estate planning. I have determined the amount in accordance with my estate plan. You will have to make these decisions for yourself. At a minimum, you should maintain ten times your annual salary in some combination of life/term insurance. Your individual circumstances will be different.

Death is a part of the circle of life. Plan for it and avoid financial surprises for your family. Use life insurance to give yourself and your family peace of mind and fulfill your estate-planning objectives.

Disability Insurance

Disability insurance covers what the name implies. If you become permanently disabled for any reason and cannot work, this type of insurance will pay you a monthly income based on the policy terms. Many experts recommend taking out disability insurance to cover a loss of income. I recommend insuring up to 60 percent of your annual salary against long-term disability. This insurance usually expires at age sixty-five when Medicare begins. By that age, you should have built up other assets to provide some peace-of-mind coverage should you have a disability later in life.

Long-Term-Care (LTC) Insurance

Long-term-care (LTC) insurance is designed to defray some of the costs of home health care, assisted living, and nursing home costs that may occur later in life. At some point, you should consider this coverage, if for no other reason than LTC being a form of asset protection. This means having LTC can avoid draining all of your assets to pay for elder care. Usually this becomes a concern around the age of sixty-five.

Unless you have a retirement fund well beyond your needs for lifelong living expenses and estate-planning provisions, LTC coverage probably makes sense. Research has projected the average retired couple will spend $250,000 on health care. Insured amounts through LTC to cover a portion of expenses (including up to five years in a nursing home with a daily cap of $200–300) are standard. Some have an annual inflation rider of 3–5 percent for an extra premium. LTC premiums are tax-deductible up to an annual limit, which is currently $4,750 for people age seventy-one or older. Long-term-care insurance should be considered as an important component of your evolving asset protection strategy after age sixty-five.

Review Beneficiary Designations

Insurance is designed to cover the unknown or at least the timing of the unknown, such as date of death. Keeping insurance coverage current and up to date is a part of your overall planning process. Make sure you maintain the desired beneficiary designations on all policies since life changes—marriages, births, deaths, divorces, or adoptions—may dictate a need to modify these from time to time.

Life insurance, like retirement accounts, has beneficiary designations. Proceeds from the policies flow to the named beneficiaries and cannot by directed differently by a will. Keep these beneficiary designations current to reflect how you want the funds distributed.

Chapter 12

529 College Savings Plans

Key Definition

529 Plan: A college savings plan that is named after the section of the IRS code that authorized them. All earnings are tax-deferred and withdrawals are tax-free as long as they are used for any educational purpose.

There is no greater gift for your children or grandchildren than the gift of an education. College education is the highest honor on this list. It is even better if it is debt free to the student. This is all possible with good planning and a 529 college savings account.

Strategy #33: Make use of college savings plans to fund future education expenses.

If you want to assist your children in paying for some or all of their college expenses, getting an early start is an absolute must. Putting savings into these tax-deferred accounts will increase the growth potential of these funds.

Individual states sponsor 529 college savings plans. At a minimum, review the plan offered by your state of residency. You can use any 529 plan from any state. Usually plans offered by your state of residency will offer parents a state tax deduction for each year they contribute. There are dollar limits to these deductions. This is one way to lower your personal state income tax. If you live in a state without a state income tax, any 529 plan is an option.

For example, if you expect to pay about $20,000 each year toward a college education, you will need to save $200 per month from the time the child is born. This can grow to $77,000 by age eighteen. This is another example of compound interest at work. Parents, grandparents, aunts, and uncles can make contributions to these plans.

Professional Management of 529 Plan

Investment professionals manage these unique savings plans. American Century, E-Trade, and Schwab & Company are a few of the named managers around the country. Remember—as long as withdrawals from these plans are used for any educational purpose, they are not taxable.

Funding a future college education through a 529 plan is superior to funding through general cash flow because of the tax-deferred benefits on earnings from the investments. Many grandparents find it desirable to fund these plans annually for their grandchildren through gifting programs.

Chapter 13

Estate Planning

Just as economics has been said to be the study of the dismal sciences, so estate planning has been labeled "duller than a rubber knife." This is because it involves planning what to do with your life's possessions, including financial assets, after your death. People generally are not keen on these types of discussions while they are alive, but they are important.

The first requirement is to put your plan in writing. It is only a hope if it is not written. Things happen in life beyond your control. Premature death, disability, or other serious health care issues may prevent you from being able to tell your family how you want your assets distributed. Be responsible and put your estate plan in writing. If you do not, the resulting lack of guidance will result in what I call a tragedy of good intentions. You owe your heirs more than this. If it is not in writing, it is not a plan—it is only a hope and a dream.

Strategy #34: Estate planning assures asset disposition in accordance with your wishes.

Everyone has an estate regardless of the amount of money involved. If you do not plan for the distribution of your assets upon your death, your state of residency has a backup plan. Why would you let your state of residency dictate your estate?

The basic components of an estate plan include the following:

- wills
- trusts
- understanding of federal estate planning guidelines for exemptions and exclusions
- monitoring future changes in tax-planning guidelines
- avoiding the potential for any state death tax penalties
- last will and testament

Wills

Wills are the cornerstone of any estate plan. These are your personal, written declarations of your intentions about disposing of your property at death. Wills are not legally enforceable until death occurs. Therefore, you can change your will anytime before death. Wills contain instructions for your personal representative. The executor is responsible for administration of your estate and must report to the probate court upon the completion of all estate matters.

Beside distribution of your assets, a will can be used to name a guardian for your minor children or others unable to care for themselves. Anytime you are planning a trip outside the continental United States, if you have children, it is best that you and your spouse complete a will prior to leaving. If you die without a will, you will have died "intestate." This is costly to your heirs and may cause your estate to pay higher estate taxes. Even if you have a trust, you should still have a will for any assets not covered by the trust.

A will is inexpensive to establish. Work with an estate-planning attorney to draft your will. Not all attorneys are qualified to work on estate matters. Be sure your choice of an attorney is a specialist in this area of the law. The will only transfers assets that you own in your name only. Property you own as a joint tenant with right of survivorship or with a named beneficiary, like life insurance, IRAs, or 401(k) accounts, cannot be transferred by a will.

Trusts

A trust complements a will. Living trusts are effective during your lifetime; a testamentary trust does not become operative until your death. Living trusts can be revocable or irrevocable. Placing assets in a trust may help shield them from future creditors if personal financial problems lead to bankruptcy or other serious debt-collection problems. Trusts are another example of an important component of an asset-protection strategy.

Exclusion Amount

The purpose of trusts includes obtaining professional management and advice, minimizing gift and estate taxes, distributing assets efficiently, and placing conditions on how and when assets should be distributed. In 2015, a deceased estate is not subject to federal estate taxes (40 percent) until the value exceeds $5.43 million, as indexed for inflation. This is called the basic exemption amount. By using a strategy known as portability, it is possible for a married couple to shield a total estate of almost $11 million from federal estate taxes in 2015. Proper planning to achieve this savings is a requirement.

Gift Tax Exclusion

The annual gift tax exclusion covers financial gifts you make during your lifetime. In 2015, each individual can make gifts of a maximum of $14,000 annually to any person tax-free. A married couple could make up to $28,000 annually in total financial gifts to a single person without tax consequences. There is no limit to the number of people you can give to under this exclusion.

State death taxes should be avoided.

Beware of state death taxes. Twelve states have separate estate taxes in addition to the federal estate tax. If your state of residency still has these taxes, consider moving to a state without them before you die. This will save considerable tax expenses for your heirs. I am serious about this recommendation. State laws change frequently so check on your state laws on this subject from time to time.

There is nothing fair about estate taxes. The assets you own have been acquired with after tax dollars meaning you have already paid taxes on the income used to purchase these assets. Until and if these death taxes are eliminated, your best hope is to do some serious estate planning to minimize the tax effect of transferring assets to those you want to have them. Work with your elected federal representatives and senators if you want to see a reduction or elimination of these estate taxes. In the meantime, coordinate with your estate-planning attorney to minimize any and all estate taxes.

When should you consider estate planning?

To make this process cost effective, a rule of thumb is you should have at least $500,000 in assets, not counting the value of your home. Other life events may require earlier planning, such as a vacation out of the country. Naming a guardian for your minor children is of paramount importance. What is the price of peace of mind for you and your spouse? The answer will tell you when to begin estate planning. Hiring an estate-planning attorney will cost an hourly fee.

Estate planning is never done. Your plan should be updated at least annually, subject to changes in your life (the birth of a child, divorce, death of a named beneficiary, move to another state for job opportunities, and other life-changing events). Congress can always change the rules regarding federal estate planning, and your estate-planning attorney should be asked to make sure your plan is in current compliance and will maximize tax efficiencies upon your death.

Chapter 14

Create Your Own Pension

Key Definitions

Immediate or Fixed Annuities: These insurance products generate income *during retirement.* These are valuable components of a lifetime income and typically guarantee a fixed or minimum return over a set period of time.

Indexed Annuities: These offer returns based on the performance of a specific market index.

Deferred Variable Annuities: These insurance products accumulate assets *before retirement.* They allow owners to invest the premium in subaccounts (similar to mutual funds). I do not recommend these for your plan.

There are two basic requirements to becoming financially prepared for retirement: saving on a regular basis and investing prudently. If either of these is not sufficient, you face the possibility of a deferred or delayed retirement.

Strategy #35: Individual responsibility for retirement is the only sure strategy.

Prepare yourself to rely on personal savings in retirement. I call this, again, the DIY approach.

The future of social security is open to debate. At a minimum, by the time you retire, there may be a means test for future benefits. The more income you have, the less you potentially will receive in social security benefits. You will probably wait longer for full social security benefits. Extending the age for full benefits to seventy would prolong the solvency of this safety net program. Do not rely on social security benefits being available when you retire. Consider whatever you may receive in social security benefits in the future to be a gift—even though you will have paid into the fund for your entire working career through social security tax deductions. Do not rely on social security for your retirement living expenses.

Strategy #36: Create your own pension.

All is not lost. You can create your own pension to provide for a lifetime of income and never outlive your money. This option is available for self-employed workers, part-time workers, full-time employees, and anyone else with a desire to provide for their financial independence.

When you retire, plan to replace 85–100 percent of your preretirement income. When the paychecks stop coming, this is what you have to live on for the rest of your life. It may sound daunting, and it will be if you have not done a good job of planning for and funding your retirement. You do not arrive at retirement age overnight; you control when it is going to happen (unless you are caught in a company downsize program, are fired, or have a serious medical condition). You have years to prepare for the day of retirement—make the most of it.

According to Fidelity Investments, by age sixty, you should have saved about six times your current annual income for retirement. This is assuming you can grow your portfolio by 5.5 percent annually, retire at age sixty-seven, and live to ninety-two. It also assumes replacing 85 percent of your preretirement income when you stop working. If you are off track, adjust one of the factors you can control (delaying your retirement date, living on less money, or finding part-time work in retirement).

Strategy #37: One type of annuity makes sense.

Immediate or fixed annuities, indexed or deferred annuities, and other longevity insurance products all have costs and risks. By giving up a lump sum of money, you lose any future capital gains treatment on profits, you cannot offset gains and losses in your portfolio, and your heirs lose any step-up in cost basis, if or when they inherit the annuity account. If you can live with these risks, then you will never run out of money.

Immediate fixed annuities can create a lifetime pension. They are a form of longevity insurance, not investments. An immediate fixed annuity has the primary purpose of generating income *during* retirement. The traditional 4 percent rule, which states that your money should last thirty years as long as you withdraw no more than 4 percent of the principal annually, can be supplemented by converting no more than 20–25 percent of your retirement assets into an immediate fixed annuity. This annuity will provide a fixed-income stream for the rest of your lifetime. Payments are usually made monthly.

Consider the purchase of an immediate fixed annuity after age seventy-five because the older you are when you purchase this product, the shorter your life expectancy and the higher the payout percentage. I would not buy an annuity with less than an 8 percent payout, meaning a combination of interest and return of principal. Using immediate fixed annuities, you are assured of never outliving your money.

Note: I am not recommending investing 100 percent of your retirement funds in an annuity. Using some percentage of those assets, no more than 20–25 percent, or a fixed dollar amount like $300,000 should be enough to generate income to cover your basic monthly expenses in retirement. This product meets the requirement of keeping it simple. You turn over a lump sum of money, and the insurance company promises to pay you a fixed amount monthly for life. There are other options available to add to an immediate fixed annuity such as an inflation rider or guaranteed full payout of your original sum invested to your heirs if you die before this has occurred. Any of these options will reduce your monthly payments to pay for the options. I recommend immediate fixed annuities as part of your overall retirement funding.

One type of annuity I prefer is the *term certain annuity*. This product provides payments for a specified period. Terms vary from three-to-twenty-year versions of this product. My choice would be a ten-to-twenty-year payout. Some fixed-term annuities can also offer a maturity amount at the end of the period. The higher monthly income you choose, the lower the maturity amount. If you die before the term certain period matures, the payments may continue to your spouse or other family members.

Social security payments are an example of an income annuity for life. Unlike payouts from a Roth IRA, annuity payments are taxed as ordinary income.

There are other types of annuities such as indexed and deferred variable annuities. These can have high expenses and poor investment performance. The brokers who sell them often earn commissions. They are used for accumulating assets *before* retirement. I do not recommend indexed or deferred-variable annuities. They are designed to buy earlier in your life and require monthly payments in the form of premiums and project to pay out funds at a later specified age, usually after seventy-five, based on some assumed investment performance.

All annuities are a form of insurance. They are insurance contracts. They are not the best investment tools for building your net worth, and they have costs such as surrender charges, commissions, and fees associated with them. Annuities can provide a high reliability of income rather than a good rate of return.

Inherent Risks of Annuities

There are several risks to consider when using an immediate fixed annuity. You pay a single premium at the time of purchase; therefore, you are giving up control over a large sum of money that you cannot access in the future. Another risk is inflation risk. The annuity pays a fixed amount monthly for life. If inflation increases, meaning the cost of living goes up, then the fixed payments will purchase less. Finally, because an annuity is an insurance product, the financial strength of the insurance company from whom you purchase the annuity is important. You do not want the insurance company to become insolvent. Look for the AM Best Company rating for the insurance company. I recommend companies with an A+ rating: the highest rating possible.

When you buy an annuity, you are going to need the income for a long time. Do not take any unnecessary risks with the purchase of an immediate fixed annuity by purchasing it from an unreliable company.

Chapter 15

Million-Dollar Retirement

Raising your retirement expectations can be uplifting and fulfilling. You should be able to save a million dollars or more for retirement *if* you start saving early. However, most people do not achieve this level of savings because of a lack of financial discipline, failure to plan, or being too busy living life and putting off any thoughts about the future. Too many people live only in the present and do not plan for the future. Good intentions are not enough; action is required. It is entirely up to you.

Build a solid retirement fund.

Here is one example of how to build a million-dollar retirement plan. This example assumes your employer offers a 401(k) plan with a match. A person who saves $7,500 per year ($625 monthly) beginning at age thirty in a 401(k), gets a $1,500 match annually, and earns 7 percent average annual returns will have $1,411,295 saved by age sixty-five. This retirement fund will generate approximately $56,000 annually for thirty years, if you limit your withdrawals to 4 percent before adjusting for inflation. To this amount add any social security, pension, or other income from investments or part-time work. You should subtract taxes if the funds are in a tax-deferred account subject to taxation upon distribution, such as a 401(k). Having at least a seven-figure fund for retirement is really only a minimum if you plan to live an active retirement life.

Build a solid retirement fund without a 401(k) plan.

Here is another example. If you fund your IRA at the maximum contribution level of $5,500 per year beginning at age thirty, continue making $5,500 contributions annually, and assume a 7 percent rate of return, you will have $872,245 by age sixty-five. This example assumes you do not have access to a 401(k) plan through your employer. Assume over the thirty-five years that other savings and investments will accumulate at the rate of at least $3,700 annually or $310 per month to fill the $128,000 gap needed to reach the million-dollar objective. At $1,000,000, you will enjoy $40,000 income annually before social security and other income if you stay with the 4 percent withdrawal rate. Funding your IRA should be your second investment decision annually—right after you fund your 401(k) plan to the maximum allowed.

Stay the course.

No matter your age, the key to reaching a long-term goal like financial independence in retirement is to identify your financial destination, chart a course to reach it, and then stay with it. Life happens, so be ready to make adjustments as needed. If your retirement plan is not in writing, it's not a plan; it is a wish.

Chapter 16

Call to Action

You can shape the life you want after your career ends. It is never too early to plan for retirement. The sooner you start saving, the more time the money has to grow. Put time on your side!

To help take control of your individual retirement plan and make the process more enjoyable than you might be expecting, I have compiled some of my most effective strategies from a lifetime of financial experience. There are no shortcuts. These strategies all come together at the intersection of investing and retirement planning.

Nobody else will care if your retirement planning is turned upside down by financial market crashes or other variables. You are the one who has to plan, execute, and deliver your personal financial independence in retirement. I have read articles describing people in their thirties and forties who have more in credit card debt than they have in savings.

Recent studies have shown that approximately 37 percent of people between fifty and sixty-five have saved less than $25,000 toward retirement. They are a disaster waiting to happen. They must live in the camp of Americans that assume the government will look after them. Reality is harsh; the federal government has made promises it cannot keep when it comes to providing a safety net of social security and Medicare health coverage. Changes are needed in both social security and Medicare to improve their sustainability. Without significant changes in the way this group of people spend, save, and invest, many of them will not be able to afford the retirement they want. You are on your own to provide for your future. Do not rely on the government to take care of you.

The good news is there are many tools available to help you in this retirement-planning process. This book is one of them; others include online retirement calculators, investment-advisory services, and websites on any subject you want to research. A few of my favorite retirement planning resources are:

- *Fidelity Retirement Income Planner:* It is free, but it is usually best to use if you are within five years of retirement.
- *Vanguard Financial Planning:* The fee is based on how much you have invested in the Vanguard family of investments.
- *Nationwide RetireSense:* It is free, but expect to pay commissions if you buy any of their investment products.
- *Schwab Real Life Retirement Services:* It is free if you have Schwab accounts.

These tools are of little value unless you access them and use them to your advantage.

Outside Resources

Lawrence J. Kaplan's *Retiring Right* is a comprehensive guide to retirement planning, yet it is written in simple language. I recommend it as a reference on this subject. Steve Vernon's *Money For Life* discusses turning your IRA and 401(k) accounts into a lifetime retirement check. Every investor should read Peter

Mallouk's *The 5 Mistakes Every Investor Makes and How to Avoid Them*. This hands-on guide to avoiding common investing mistakes is easy to follow.

Conclusion

I have outlined the topics and strategies that I believe can help you to achieve financial independence. If these topics stimulate your thoughts, then further research may be necessary on your part. This book has been written as a self-help tool to facilitate planning in one area of your financial life. With this book, you can walk the talk of investing and retirement planning.

Whether you are twenty, thirty, forty, or fifty, investing is most successful when you have specific goals in mind. I believe strongly in the DIY approach to investing. At some point, you may want to consider hiring a professional money manager and/ or a financial adviser. Expect to pay fees of 1 percent of total assets annually for assets under management (AUM). Usually, a threshold of $250,000 in investable assets (not counting the value of your home) may be required to engage professional management efficiently.

As outlined in this book, your investment portfolio should contain both equities and fixed-income products. John Bogle, the legendary founder of the Vanguard Group and a strong index fund advocate, advises that your age should match your bond exposure. He believes if you are fifty, a safe, conservative balance is to have 50 percent of your portfolio in bonds and 50 percent in equities. Equities can consist of index funds, mutual funds, and individually selected stocks in companies that you have high confidence in for their financial strength and market dominance.

The fixed-income side of your portfolio can be spread among US Treasuries (high safety and low yield), corporate bonds, and a few in between. Well-respected bond funds like Dodge & Cox

(DODIX) or iShares Lehman Aggregate Bond (NYSE: AGG) offer diverse exposure to the total bond market with below-average fees. The equity portion of your portfolio should contain a mix of growth-oriented companies and dividend-paying stocks. Several of my current favorite long-term dividend payers are Coca-Cola (KO), Abbott Labs (ABT), Johnson & Johnson (JNJ), Altira (MO), and McDonald's (MCD). More diversified funds like the best-in-class ETF iShares Dow Jones Select Dividend (DVY) are also good additions to any portfolio. These names are just a few when it comes to investment recommendations, but I wanted to share some of my personal best choices.

Key Dates for Retirement Planning

- *Early Twenties:* Get started saving and investing and make both a habit. Put both activities on autopilot, start an IRA, and/or participate in a company-sponsored 401(k) plan.
- *50:* Eligible for "catch-up" contributions annually to both IRAs and 401(k) plans of $1,000 and $5,500, respectively.
- *59-1/2:* Eligible to take penalty-free distributions from most retirement accounts.
- *65:* Eligible for Medicare health coverage (mandatory).
- *67:* Full retirement age for social security benefits for persons born after 1960.
- *70-1/2:* Required minimum distributions from regular IRA.
- *Beyond Retirement Age:* Enjoy your well-earned peace of mind and do the things you enjoy most because you have achieved financial independence.

When it comes to managing your investments, active monitoring and maintaining your portfolio is more advantageous than ignoring your portfolio. Buy and hold does not mean to ignore what is happening around you that may have a negative impact on the performance of your investment portfolio.

Active Monitoring and Maintaining

- Review your investment statements monthly (and no less than quarterly).
- Rebalance annually to ensure your asset allocation remains consistent with your target. Any deviation of >10–20 percent indicates it is time to rebalance the equity and fixed-income mix.
- Avoid market timing because you end up leaving the market too early and reentering the market too late. I recommend staying fully invested.
- Update your plan for life changes as they occur and remain flexible. As you age, you may have a change in risk tolerance or change priorities as your family grows.
- Don't overmanage your portfolio. You are not a day trader. Too many transactions can generate commissions, taxes, and other expenses that reduce your investment returns.

Strategy #38: Take active ownership of your future.

Can I afford to retire? This is the ultimate question you must be able to answer. This book is like your automobile's owner's manual because you are the owner of your investment and retirement-planning strategies. Take active ownership of your future by using this guideline as a resource to troubleshoot various questions or deviations from expected results. If you make your plan enduring yet adaptable, you can enjoy the peace of mind of achieving financial independence for a fulfilling retirement. If you have successfully implemented the strategies in this book, the answer to the question of being able to afford to retire is yes.

What is my best advice for your retirement planning?

Put time on your side by starting to save and invest early. After you launch your career, continue working up to full retirement age (at a minimum). To reach your financial goals, you may have to work even longer. Maintain active contributions to both IRA and 401(k) savings plans as long as you work. Do not take social security until full retirement age of sixty-seven (or later). Only take the required minimum distributions (RMD) from your regular IRA to be sure you do not outlive those funds. Consider following the 4 percent rule for distributions from a Roth IRA or other retirement funds. Buy an immediate fixed annuity with a small percentage or fixed-dollar amount of your total retirement fund that will pay an amount to cover basic monthly expenses. Relax and enjoy retirement. You have planned for it, and now you have achieved it.

Good planning equates to good results. Knowledge is power when you put what you have learned from this book into action.

This is not the end. It is only the beginning of a lifetime journey! You can achieve financial independence with financial discipline. Enjoy implementing the strategies outlined in this book in your own way and within your own comfort zone. You will be happy with the results. Put time on your side by starting to save and invest early and stay the course over the rest of your life.